Kim Hiles

AS THE DUST SETTLES

AUSTIN MACAULEY PUBLISHERS™

LONDON • CAMBRIDGE • NEW YORK • SHARJAH

A CIP catalogue record for this title is available from the British Library.

ISBN 9781035872343 (Paperback)
ISBN 9781035872350 (ePub e-book)

www.austinmacauley.com

First Published 2024
Austin Macauley Publishers Ltd®
1 Canada Square
Canary Wharf
London
E14 5AA

Kim Hiles enjoys writing about her journey of self-discovery. She is the author of *PE for the Soul, Walks with Strays,* and co-authored *Little Wonders.* Her debut book of poetry published by Austin Macauley Publishers, *Moments as They Come,* offers solace and understanding for those experiencing the empty nest transition. Her second book of poetry, *As the Dust Settles,* is about what comes next and offers hope and new beginnings.

Kim's books touch on various themes such as addiction, depression, anxiety, career, and animals as healers, to name a few. Kim's story is one of struggle and self-compassion that leads to abundant self-awareness and personal growth. Her memoir is shared with enjoyable poetic expression in short story format.

As an educator for 20 years, Kim has worked with both children and adults teaching social & emotional learning, physical education, as well as behavioral coaching.

Kim pens a blog and enjoys empowering others on their quest for self-discovery.

Go to *www.kimhiles.com* for more information.

I would like to thank my mom Sonja for all of her support and my husband Will who taught me to stay true to my own style. I am so grateful for my family and my life. Thank you to all who have supported my work. Life is such a journey.

Moving On

You can't think of a reason
Nothing in particular stands out
But it's been building for a while
As you wait for clarity

You've altered your perspective
Changed things up
Brought fresh ideas
Kept it interesting

A crisis
The wakeup call
The painful release of old
The grieving

The pain goes on
It's endless so it seems
Just long enough to get the needed message
The clothing needing to be shed

The grief feels heavy
Until it doesn't
I know what I need to do
It's exhilarating and exciting
Until it's not

As the dust settles
From the onslaught of new beginnings
Endings
A peace moves in
Fear moves out
I stand tall with my arms wide open
"I'm ready!" I declare
As I trust the process of my life

The Doorway

Excitement is in the air
For years thinking is this it?
Depression here and there
Hanging on for dear life

A wakeup call
One too many
But just enough to hear
Clarity stared at me
Couldn't look away

New ideas took shape
Anticipation returned
Fear has a way of returning
But new and practiced skills keep it hidden

New Year's Eve day
How is that so?
It feels like spring
Rebirth I declared

Every experience prepares you
For what is next
Take a deep breath
Give thanks

Step through the door

Old Garments are Shed

A raggedy old woman
With smelly old garments
Weighing her down
How does she stand it?

Comfortable she spits
Don't care I hear
She does this forever
Or so it seems

Then one day
The old coat hangs off of her shoulder
Intrigued she pushes it to the floor
She is light as a feather

Dances like an excited ballerina
Acts like she is 6
Innocent she appears
Not a care, she dares

She feels exposed
Walking on eggshells
Waiting for the other shoe to drop
Needed new ones anyway

She takes one step at a time
Into the unknown
Her face looks more soft
Scared but hopeful

Pen to Paper

It's so simple
Breathe I say
Quiet the mind
Let the pen talk

Guidance from within
Will never lead you astray
Turn the mind off
Allow the pen to be the instrument

It can be anything
A rattle, drum, dance
Allow yourself to be led
Don't hold your breath

Takes practice
Especially for the controlling one
Turn the mind off
Surrender to the moment

One second at a time
Bring it back
Try again
Smiles and love will tiptoe in

Easier with time

In the Air

It's a trusting of the process
One minute I'm out the door
The sky is brilliant, orange and red
Delirious laughter ensues

What's that?
A change of perspective it seems
I am showing up day by day with excitement
The old no longer feels old

A trick is it?
What is up and what is down?
I am clear
I am not

Joy can come to any situation
Anger and sadness can keep us stuck
Smiling has become the norm
It's an acceptance of sorts

Trusting the process
What's in the air today?
As long as happiness is my companion
I cannot fail

What will be will be

Tightrope

I am balancing on a tightrope
The scent on one side is lavender
The music makes me high

The feeling of delight is breathtaking
Moves me to tears
I sing loud
Everything is bright

On the left, I hear voices
"What if?" they say
I could crash to the ground
With a simple breeze
Or unsuspecting hurricane

The balancing act is real
The feeling of powerlessness
With things beyond our control
Life is like that, you see

Anchoring in love
Makes me grounded
No longer walking, suspended

Centered and strong

Meditation Bliss

The morning moment
All is as it should be
In the stillness
No regrets

Girl dancing with the bouncy ball
Air balloons in the sky
Here there and everywhere
Rolled into one

What will be will be
Beating up on self no more
Trust in each moment
Hand held to the sky

Ocean waves and endless sand
I walk through that door
Breathe in the experience
Bliss, galore

A smile appears
Excited and at peace
A life lived well
Second act appears

Or is it the sixth?

A Crumbling of Sorts

A tearing down of a prior life
The joy it brought for so long
I taught others to find their joy
Never settle for "work"

It's a mission, a passion, an excitement beyond compare
It's a life doing what you love
Providing all needs in return
And when the end is reached, you'll know

When it becomes static
The years blend into one
A drudgery, a going-through-the-motions
A nudge may be felt
Sometimes a sledgehammer to the head happens instead

We will know
We get back to going within
Listening to the small voice
Paying attention to details
In words, articles, sensations, automatic writing

The way is clear
Or not
But we know change is taking place
We go to the edge of the diving board
Jump
Into the unknown
With faith

A Vivid World

It's always been so
I could ride in a boat
Stare up at the sky
Take a trip across the world
Wonder if I could fly

Let's go to the beach
Warm sand at my feet
Sun felt on my back
Basking in its sweet embrace

Sitting in the baby pool
Drink in my hand
I am at a tropical resort
Flamingos standing tall on the grass

A smile on my face
I'm there in my mind
I can go anywhere
So I stay here

And relish this vivid world
With scents and colors
The blue and white sky
It's here, there and everywhere
As am I

Dancing Leaves

Sitting with Zelda by my side
Looking at the murky water
What's that sound?
I look, can't find the source

Stillness
The yellow butterflies fly around me
I watch their dancing flight
Is that a crow? I turn to look

The smile now comes
Grinning ear-to-ear
I'm in the zone
Nature symphony playing just for me

"There is so much life out here"
I say this out loud
In a smooth awestruck way
I snap some photos and take a video to remember

The sweetness of this moment
Captured for all eternity

As I walk slowly home, I hear footsteps behind
It's a swirl of leaves
The wind carrying them
In step with mine

They twirl home with me
On the sidewalk across the street
The smile never leaves my face
As their journey ends

"Thank you, my dancing leaves"

Surrender

When the buried truth
Is finally allowed to shine
The flashlight exposes the crime
It is in that vision
We see it was not worth the dime

It is our resistance that made it so powerful
Our need for happiness, bells and whistles
Yet there is a sweetness that is felt
In the release of knowing

It must not be so painful
Drudgery at its finest
But an honest reflection between two lost souls
In their remembrance and truth

A new partnership is formed
Lighter and less hurtful
It's an authentic beginning
The future unknown

The storm is moving out to sea
The waves are gentle and soft at my feet
The calm sky and the scent of sea air
Brings a gentleness to my heart
In this moment of peace

A Swirl of Energy

Can you help?
A little hand folds into mine
The adult, breathless with questions
The swirl of energy
It's hot, cold, unmoving, spinning

The phone rings
The door knocks
The little bodies move in and out
There, not here, can you lend a hand?

Don't have time for parties
Can't you come and say hello?
Little innocent asks with wonder
Too busy, putting out fires
Maybe another day

Breathe in and out
Slowly
Crisis
Calm on the outside
How many can fit in this room?

Still have work to do when the littles leave
Process
Still processing
Tears, exhaustion, done

No longer want or need this
It's time to move on
Trying to finish strong
Leave no stone unturned

I've never been more ready
To leap
Like a bird taking flight
Up…into the sky

Summer

Letting years of service go
The future is unknown
I have what it takes
Offers here and there

But I don't need to jump
Just sit in the silence
Contemplate it all
Heart lead

The boy graduated
College years flew
Coming home
Plans being made

There is a quiet serenity
In a life well lived
Individual lives changed
A sprinkle here and there

I'm not nearly done
But the scenery is changing
It hit me today
As I sat in silence
Feeling waves gently tugging me below
The surface

Blues

Such profound sadness
Is that the root?
Of the daggers, I feel
Throw them I must

Anger all the way
That's what I was told
That's your description?
Maybe there is a truth

Below the surface
Is a churning
A bubbling
Red hot like lava

Where does it come from?
What does it want?
Freedom from fear
A release into the unknown

I sit in silence
Feel the pain
As I wonder
Who I am

Gold

Do you know your own value?
I thought I did
Innocent and excited
I leapt toward a dream

Fear must have taken root
Did you not feel you could?
Did it win?
Defeated and crushed

I settled for less
I think that might be true
But I tell myself otherwise
The outcome is anger
A slow painful death

The pulsating lingers
A heartbeat steady
I feel it in my head
Break free it says

To what?
Some things cannot be won
When you put others first
But your voice comes out big, bad and strong
Or so it seems
Hear me it says

To what end?
I wonder
I feel split in half
A constant battle of thieves
Each shouting to be heard
A standoff of sorts
Each hanging on til the bitter end

Pool

My son has grown
Graduated college
At the water park today
Watching families just starting out

Those were the days

Feeling wistful in a way

Playing the right music
Bringing me back
To the years before the kid
"Free falling" he sings

It happens to everyone
Cycle of life
A trip, I think
A smile on my face

Doing an activity I love
Swimming to the current
A smile
Present

Social Wonder

Inept I say
Never quite got it
In groups, awkward
Hang onto that one

So I can survive the moment
Too close?
Push them away
Too far? Why bother

Solitary moments are free
Of subtle messages
Made up or their own
Doubting be gone

It ought to come naturally
Moments with others
An authentic telling
Sharing the moment

I generally don't seek it
Allow it to come
Intensity is not for everyone
Acceptance is the aim

In Spite of Me

I jumped off the cliff
But a branch was there
I grabbed it
Stopped the freefall

When soul and self come together
It's a coming to terms
One sees all
Can guide in a more gentle way

I had an idea
A dream, if you will
Reality hit, and with that,
Came clarity

Oh I know
I'm a speaker on follow your dreams
It continues
In a more gentle and gradual way

I'm excited about the changes I did make
New beginnings in the fall
And creativity continues
When I feel the desire

My inner guide is always looking out
Can see the big picture
So I take the path of least resistance
Filling my cup with ease

Break Free

The urge is massive
It starts with a decluttering
The closet
Garage
Extra weight

What am I really letting go of?
What chain binds me?
Self-imposed you know
It's brewing, percolating if you wish

It's ok to change things up
Go back to the somewhat familiar
It's a charging
A force growing
Getting stronger

I will know when it's time
There will be no turning back
Lightness is what I hear
A feather floating
Various destinations will appear

My Sister

The greatest inspiration I know
Doesn't worry about things of old
A future unknown
No

She lives in the moment
Enjoys each day to its fullest
Doing things she loves
Appreciating always what is

No matter what is going on in her body
She has not a care in the world
She smiles in wonder
At the landscape, the music, the adventure she is on

She has always been my go-to
How to be in this world

I've never been able to master
The lust of living she has
Escape comes easily to me
Life passes by….

The words hit me hard today
"I just go through each day…enjoying everything."

A pause

A smile

Can I?

Really, it's Forward

The sun shimmers through the trees
A wise man said
You're not going backward
It's a spiral
You're moving forward

So many gifts
Stronger and more wise
An appreciation for the simple things
Dance with the students
Yoga journey to the earth

This is the shiny object today
My focus may change again
Shining a spotlight
On all the other gifts
Channeled projects I could say

A release is felt today
A celebration of the path chosen
A gentle reminder of all that's been accomplished
A little smile appears, a smirk you'd say

Celebrate the little victories
See the light in all the crevices
Breaking through
Reminding us of our worth

Simplicity

It happens to most
A yearning for simplicity
No bells and whistles
Diamonds in the sky

Fame and fortune fall away
Good health, well-being and enlightenment
Are the catch of the day
Affirmed daily, enjoying life's simplicity

Aging can be a beautiful thing

Daily meditations
Positivity chosen
A smile and a thanks
Begin the day

As the sun rises
Taking my breath away
Snapping the photo
Etched into my heart forever

Touching just one person is enough
I contributed positively
Isn't that enough?
The way of peace

Showing up
Grateful for the day
Giving in some way
Love grows

Morning Rush

In the morning rush
As I sit for a moment and ponder
The winding path
And feeling complete

You see, I took a leap
But only landed on a ledge
"Where are you going?" the whisper asked.
You've stayed so long for a reason

It's not complete as I thought
More to be done
So I jumped back up
And landed on a different path

I've always been looked after
In spite of myself
And as doubts swirled inside
A branch was given

I ended up back to the beginning
Of the original path
But it looks so different now
This is what I'm supposed to do

Heed the calls
You never know where you end up
The path meanders
Sometimes back to the beginning
But different

More vibrant in all its colors
The glimmers of light through the leaves
Brings a fresh perspective
A knowing
All is as it should be

A Simple Smile

I mow the grass
Smiling
Clipping the vines
A smile

A simplistic life these days
Not wanting or needing much
A work week
Filled with movement and passion

A Friday night
Coffee in hand
Sleeping in I think
Never do

These are the moments
Simplicity
A presence of joy
Happy to be alive

The moon was vast
Followed me to work yesterday
In awe
The day started with a smile
It's how it ended too

Dragonfly

Sitting on the porch
A dragonfly appeared

As if to say "hi"
He did a little dance
A zig and a zag
A face-to-face meetup

My eyes followed the sequence

Time stood still
As he paused mid-flight
A greeting of sorts

Then moved away quickly
As I laughed in delight

Small Stuff

The days become more peaceful
Things once so serious
Become now a speck
In the tapestry of life

Oh how silly it now seems
How intense was I

It's a subtle change I've noticed
Things I now let go

Joy is now the mission
Sharing it inevitable

Sky, sun, moon, trees
Rainbow colored clouds
With shapes causing me to stare
In an open-mouthed smile

The way is clear

The Sea is Calm

There is a storm out at sea
But the sun is shining here
The ocean is calm
The breath moves in rhythm
With the gentle swaying of the water

Found my groove
What I love, yet didn't know the extent
It was a long fight
Planned to be someone else
But I looked right in front of me
And the answer appeared from the deepest depth

Joy has returned to the full extent
A surrendering of the present
A celebration of gifts received
And a giving in return
For I need nothing from you
Your joy is mine

Creativity continues in sync with the waves
It's an authentic celebration of self
Expression is being alive
That's enough

How Much?

Every day we wake up
We have a choice
Is this going to be the best day?
Or the worst?

When you connect to the pure essence
Of which we are all a part
You recognize the illusion
Of fear, separation, distraction, disease

Pure unconditional love
Never-ending
Unlimited
All that is

An experience not from this world
But available to us
When we tap into it
The pure light of you

Me

We

How much did I love today?

Wonderment

The stars are shining bright
Just like mid-July
Summers of old
Contentment bubbling over

I can bring it back
Like a flick of the switch
Body has not aged
My heart and mind are there

With age comes wisdom
Enough to see
It really doesn't matter
Being love, and giving love is a life well lived

The ripples spread
Trickle down to our young
Passed to many
Forever lived

They are creating their bliss
Moment to moment
Distractions and drama thrown into the mix
The recipe of life

And in the end
They too will see the wonderment of their lives
It's simplicity
Of the magical moments

Sweet Spot

You're not doing it for them
But for you
It's a freedom of sorts
Sweet is the game

The acknowledgement is extra
The icing on the cake
The realization driving home
Alone with my thoughts

The wisdom and peace
Come from a life well lived
The ups and the downs
The seesaw of life

I wrote a letter to life once
Asking for all the things
It turned out
I just needed to look over my shoulder

Nothing changed but I
And it was through living
Fighting
Growing
Sharing

The beating of my heart

I found my voice

I See

I hug myself a lot
As the tears tickle my cheek

You don't know
But I'm sure you have your own war stories

I go back to that moment
In that apartment back in the day

I couldn't see beyond my pain
When will it end?

Today I see that girl
I wave through the window

I tell her
You'll be alright!

Look at me now
Standing tall and proud

I walked through the fire
I did that, you'll see

Take my hand
It's a beautiful world

She does this I know
Because I'm here today

Goals, Really?

No, not me I said
Motivational talks, nah
I do what feels right in the moment
Intent is the word of the day

How's that working out?
In some areas, great
In others
Not

It resonated with me today
Researching here and there
Commit
Oh no, that word

I fight it
For it brings up battles
Long gone
Out to sea

But maybe there is some truth
To what was always said
I'll give it a try
I'll make my bed

Falling

Shingles comes again
The next day a fall
Three injuries, make that four
If you include the other pain

You ever feel like something's out to get you?
How many times have I hurt my ribs?
I say it happens for a reason, but why?
No need, I say, find another way
To get my attention

I just said to the boy
I don't want to hurt my ankle, let's play there
10 minutes later I'm falling to the ground
Ankle in pieces, or so it feels

Enough with the cruel jokes
The hurting for a point
Is it necessary I ask?
I once said a fluttering will do
Do I not heed the call?

Ok, I'll slow down
Watch where I'm going
Take time for me
Pamper when needed
And let the pesky guilt go, really go

It's what I say
But will I?

Magic Dust

Did you ever
Sail across the sea
Talk to a fly
A bird
Or I

I'm here as you
And the sea creatures
Land ones
And air

Each living life
Making it through a day
Closing chapters
Beginning anew

What's your world like?
I'm curious as you
Do you leap tall buildings
Or stumble in the dark?

A little of both I surmise
We are all magic dust
Perceiving our world of dreams
In a body perhaps too
Or not

Experiencing
Is what we have in common
Amazing don't you think?
To come up with such wonder
Bored we are not

The Highs and Lows

It gets to be too much sometimes
One day walking on air
Then literally crashing to the ground

Life is so beautiful
Ugly
Freeing
Confining

All of us experience it
To varying degrees
While we are made of the same stuff
Our chemistry is vastly different

We all have our own unique challenges
Even when I feel I'm the only one
The only thing you can do
Is to get back up
And with help if needed

For all things pass

Like the leaf falling off the tree
Blowing in the wind
Captured by the river
Flowing downstream

It's sad
And glorious
It's life in its fullest

Cloudy Sky

When the cloud looms
And the days are darker
I want to hide
Cry

It's inevitable
The comings and goings
Of darkness
When something disrupts my life

This time it was a fall
An illness
How some can move through tall
With me, I make myself small

But I tell myself each time
This too shall pass
It always does
But I just gotta keep showing up

Simple

And not

Refuge

It's a prison
A refuge
The place I must return
When I've been out too long

People
Places
Experiences
I welcome

Yet the inner alarm rings
And let me know
When it's time to return
I love it, I hate it
But it's all mine

Many times, it's true
I experience life's greatest treasures
The feeling-state intense
Alone in my backyard

The places I go

The Visitor

Did you ever feel
You were a speck of dust
Floating in the wind
The pines
Beckon

The scents are strong
A wintery aroma
Bounces around
Lands on a vine

A crow nearby
Calling
Always a friend
Comforting
Making the heart sing

Here there and everywhere
Belonging nowhere
a visitor
Observing
Sometimes lonely

Her Life

She has a thing
But the courage is felt
By anyone in her presence
What she has lived through
Takes your breath away
How does she do it?
I ponder

She always sees the positive
Others have it worse
I am content
I look outside, here at this window
I am happy

Looks not at yesterday
Nor tomorrow too
But is 100% alive
In this moment
And is thankful

Simplicity
Positivity
Gratitude
She is my hero

Synchronicity

There comes a time
The pieces all fall together
You know who you are
And who you wish to be

Your guides above celebrate
She said YES they declare
The pieces all fit
They leap in all directions

A ping of light there
Over there
Here
Everywhere

They have always been working for you
Accepting your truth moment to moment
But when they heard the call
They jumped into action
Allowing magic to take shape

For she said yes to life
To why she came here
She celebrated who she is
The universe dances in delight

Synchronicity appears

Tattoo

Let age not define you
I get excited, come up with plans
Then the pesky voice beckons
What now?

You're too old it says

I smile and whisper back
Nice try
I'm getting a tattoo today
Who cares if my muscles are sore?
I feel it more and more

It's an inner battle for sure
But conversations to self
Inner reckonings
Decide
Who and what will I be today?

The sun is out
I'm young in heart
What joy to be alive!

The image going on my arm
A memory of summers past
Lying in the field
Looking up at the dark and vast space
Shooting stars
Beautiful
Bliss

Even then the voice said it wouldn't last
Back to school soon
But I turned my attention back to the moment
Looked up at the night sky
As this memory etched into my soul
And now body
Forever

Winter Wonderland

As the wind howls
Through the pane
The chill calls
The darkness deep
There is life

The freezing rain may come
Winter wonderland a possibility
Unsettling thoughts form
Cold

Yet deep down
Unseen
Sleeping, not dead
The stillness was needed
Creating life yet to bloom

It will gain strength
Quietly grow
And when it's replenished its energy
Fed it's soul

It will become

Mountain

The image came to me in meditation
The symbol of love
Is a girl standing tall
Arms open wide
At the top of a mountain

Possibly because I never gave up
Even when I wanted to slip under the covers
And melt into the dark cave of my mind
Asleep for eternity

I got out of bed
Braved the light poking through the curtains
Beckoning me

She stands proud
With a smile on her face
Tears of joy washing down her cheeks
She knows what she's been through

It's a reminder that when the clouds form
And the shadow calls from the cave
It's a comfort after all
My trusted companion
I can show her the image of the girl
At the top of the mountain

And the sweetness that is felt
Will impart strength
And a spring in my step
As I continue on my journey
With patience and love

Freedom

Focus on your heart
Imagine it filling with unconditional love
Feel it expand
The love spreading
Experience the freedom felt
In seeing love/spirit in everyone
Notice how light you are
And witness the love spreading
Person to person
By spontaneous acts of kindness

Shared Meal

I once shared a meal with a homeless man
I sat on the park bench
Asked him about his life
And how he came to be here in this moment

My eyes filled as he shared his story
His truth
His heartache
His pain

I thought of him today
It's been too long since I've done something like that
I remember taking him out to lunch
An occasional stare

I don't remember giving advice
Just two souls
Being present
Sharing in the moment

We sure like to remember our mistakes
And forget the times love has guided us

A Poet

Sitting in an after-school club
Modern dance
A poem about flowers and trees
And what they need to live

It's a blurry memory
Never forgotten

Took a different path
The woods were filled with danger
At different times
And branched off
Some not taken

Eventually, it led me back
To the solitary girl
Who likes to dance
Write poetry

A celebration of who I am
At the core

I Want To

Take a walk under a midnight sky
Gaze upon the stars

Snap a photo of the butterfly dance
As flowers bloom

Camera in hand
A fiery sky

Clouds puffed
Like a mountain peak in the distance

With Zelda by my side
Observing, noticing, being

This is the peace I seek

Not busy work weeks
Full of must-dos

I want to wake up when I'm ready
And explore my surroundings

Write poetry

Is that too much to ask?

We

We are all not so different
Noticing, comparing, judging

We beat up on ourselves
When we are less than perfect too

We judge others harshly
Among so-called friends or even to ourselves

Aiming, striving, having to be the best
It must be so or we'll disappear

It's when we see or read the struggles of others
We realize we're the same

And if we can agree on that
We have found common ground

And that's the start
To the greater good
For it will either bring connection
Or remind us we're not that bad

And then

Self-love can take root

Heart Freedom

When I connect to my heart
Breathe in love
Gratitude
A happy memory

I may not notice right away

But in time I see

The stars now aligned
A peace washes over me
Past irritations blow away in the breeze
Joy comes back swiftly

And I look up at the galaxy
And I smile

The wrinkles of joy
Etched on my face
Are a testament
Of a full life and no regrets

Opening my heart
That's the cure
I have the opportunity
To choose it every day

Directly in Front

We all have dreams
What if…
And we try
And we build
And we create
And we wait

We throw our hands in the air

We look at what's come easy
What is directly in front of us
On our path
Calling to us
Take my hand

We surrender

Take her hand
Step forward and feel the joy return
Maybe the timing is not right
Maybe prior to birth, we made a pact
And so we accept what is

Dream another day

Unless

We are living the dream

The First Bud

It's been a year since I observed
Amazed
At the life out here
Springtime flowers, bees, butterflies, birds

I got a glimpse today
Of life coming back
The first buds

How has it been a year?
Soaking up the sun
I sat, amazed

In a few months
My son will move out
Post college life
Ready to start anew

Bittersweet

Such memories flash before my eyes
As we both prepare for the next act
There is an anticipation
A future not yet carved

Ideas are forming
Ready to take root
From where I stand today
I once imagined
From a dream

An idea

The Canvas

We are the author
Painter
Of our own life

Put brush to paper
And see where it leads

Don't like the direction it's taking?
Turn that rock into an exquisite diamond
From fire to an eagle taking flight

At any point along the way
We can reshape our masterpiece

Breathe
Close your eyes
And see a new story
Landscape

You are the creator

Star

May your night
Be made for you

Your tomorrow
A dream come true

May the light that you are
Be reflected in that star

That is you

Shine on!

Groundhog Day

Wake up
Wash
Rince
Repeat

There is no time
Past
Future

But this moment
Now

Redundancy is the word of the day

And yet joy is an ongoing feeling
Gratitude and appreciation for all I have
All I do

Speaking truth
Allowed the right doors to open.

It's a good life

Act 10

We are different characters
In so many stories
Making it up as we go along

Nothing is written in stone
The script can change at any time
As life can take on new meaning

At times we question the direction
But realize we cannot see the big picture
Sometimes the act prepares us for the next scene

The camera shifts its focus
A whole new character emerges
Bringing new life

Blessed

In the end
Love what you do
If you don't, ask
"Who am I and what do I want?"

It doesn't have to define you
Or be earth-shattering
We take on many roles
Playing different characters after all

It can be as simple as a mind shift
A change in perspective
Or different direction
Sometimes both

Are you able to have fun?
Do you touch others in positive ways?
Do you feel passion?
What keeps showing up?

I realized today
While at a dance with the youngsters
This voice whispered to me
"You make a difference"

I saw a blast from the past
He was grown up
And beaming

My life is blessed